This book belongs to

_____

You Are an Artist!

By Jennifer Stolzer

to Dawson

You ARE an Artist!

©2021 Jennifer R.Stolzer, LLC

All rights reserved under international and pan-american copyright conventions. No part of this book may be used or reproduced in any manner without written permissions.

ISBN: 9798496832991
www.jenniferstolzerbooks.com

To the young artists of the world.

Keep expressing yourselves!

"You are not an artist," they said to me.

"You aren't good enough."

"You're not special enough."

"You should stop trying."

But just because they don't like my art doesn't mean it's bad.

It may not be perfect,
but perfect is not the goal of art.

As long as I keep practicing,
I'll keep getting better.

Making art is an adventure.

And the journey is just as important as where it ends!

When I make art,
it comes from my heart.

Making art helps me feel good.

It lets me share my ideas.

My art is important because I am the one who made it.

Whether it's drawing and painting,

or sculptures and crafts,

or taking photos,
or buildng buildings,

art can be anything
as long as you make it!

"You are not an artist," they said, but they are wrong!

I am an artist, because I create!

And that's why YOU are an artist, too!

THE END

Never stop creating!
Whether it's with pencils,
or crayons, or clay, or blocks, or glue,
or glitter, or clothes, or jewelry,
or cooking, or baking, or dancing,
or anything else, express yourself!

Keep creating. Don't listen to anyone
who tells you to give up, or says that you aren't
good enough. They are wrong!

As long as you look, tell, imagine,
create, feel, and share

You are an Artist!

Did you enjoy You Are an Artist? Check out You Are a Writer and help support the St. Louis Writers Guild!
www.jenniferstolzerbooks.com

Made in the USA
Monee, IL
03 November 2021